Fish Are Animals

CONCEPT SCIENCE

Written by Judith Holloway and Clive Harper
Illustrated by Doss

Fish live in water.
Fish can breathe
under water.

Humans can't breathe
under water
without air tanks.

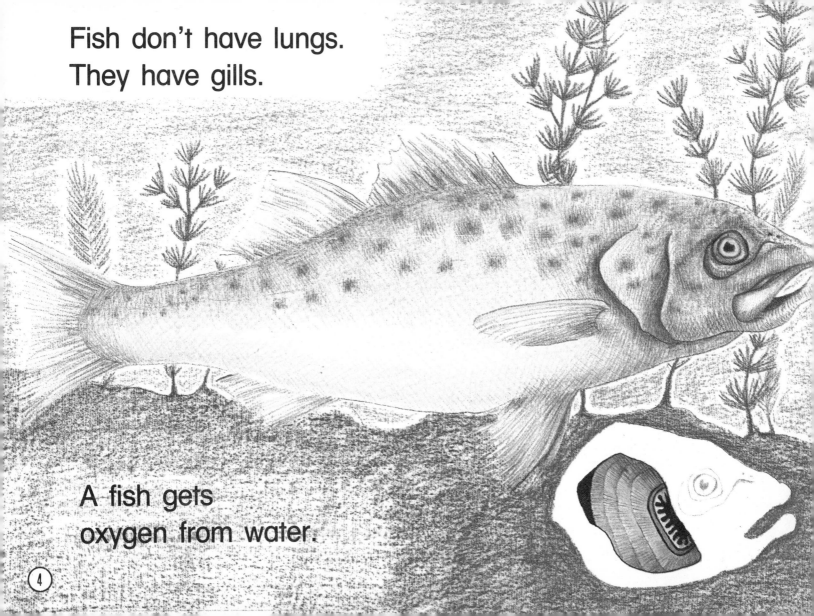

Fish don't have lungs.
They have gills.

A fish gets
oxygen from water.

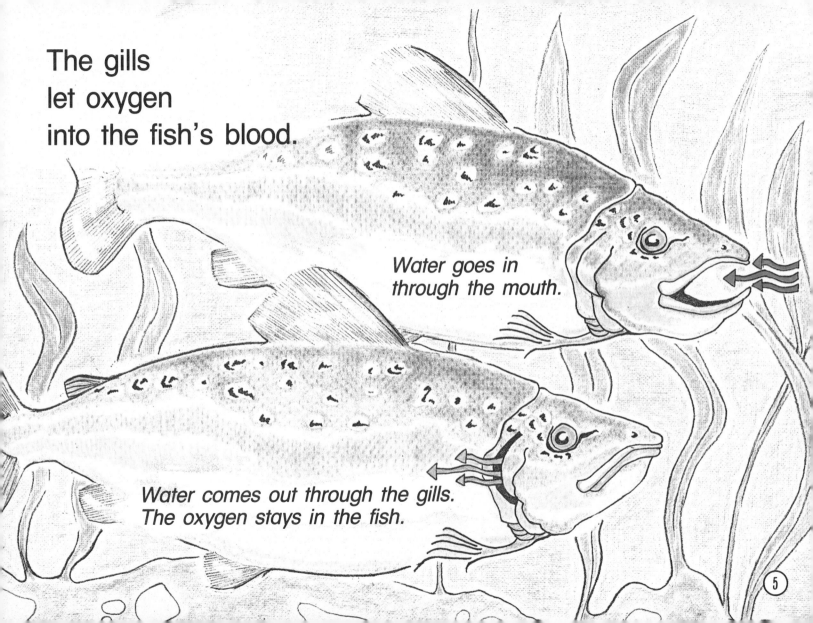

The gills
let oxygen
into the fish's blood.

*Water goes in
through the mouth.*

*Water comes out through the gills.
The oxygen stays in the fish.*

Fish are cold-blooded,
like reptiles and amphibians.

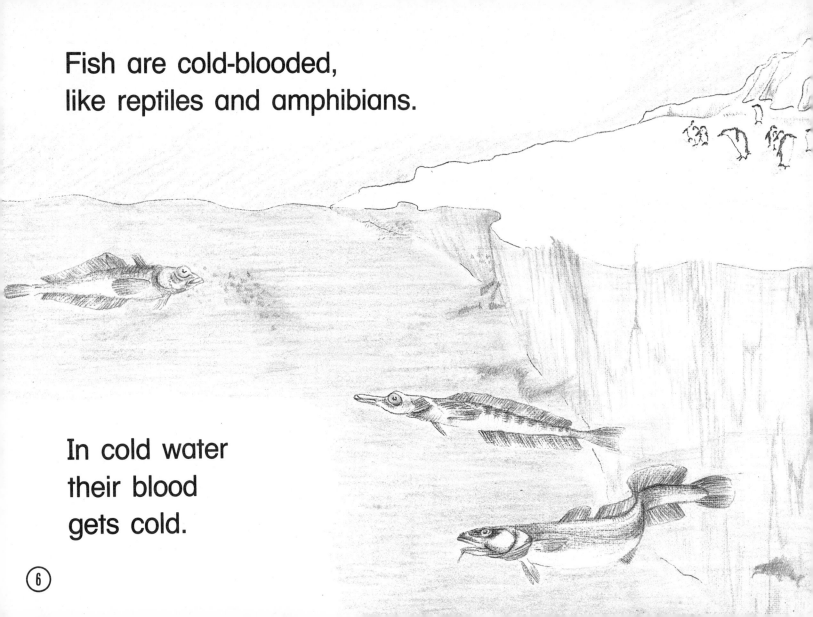

In cold water
their blood
gets cold.

In warm water
a fish's blood
gets warm.

Fish get weak
if they are put in water
that is colder or hotter than they are used to.

All fish have backbones.

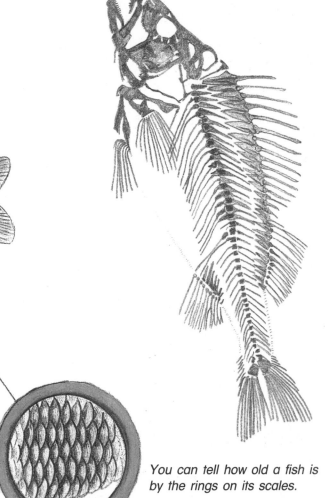

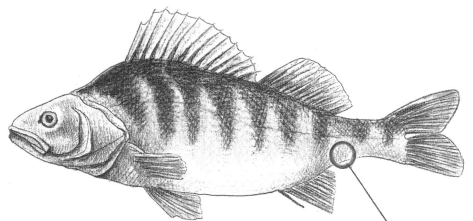

Most fish are covered
with scales
which help
to protect them.

*You can tell how old a fish is
by the rings on its scales.*

Most fish swim
by twisting their bodies.
The tail fin
pushes the water
from side to side.

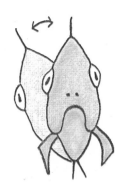

The other fins
are for steering.

Most baby fish hatch
out of eggs.
Lots of these eggs
get eaten by adult fish.

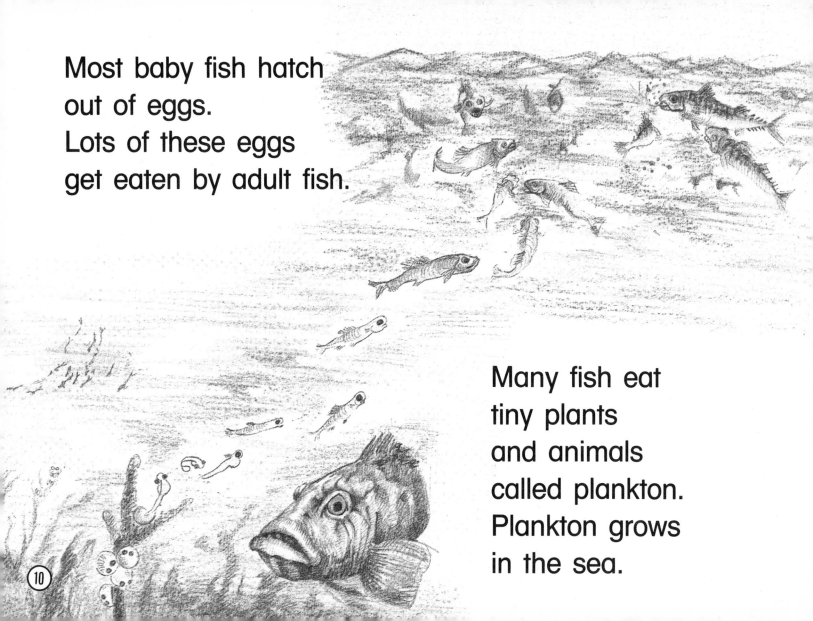

Many fish eat
tiny plants
and animals
called plankton.
Plankton grows
in the sea.

Some fish eat
other fish.

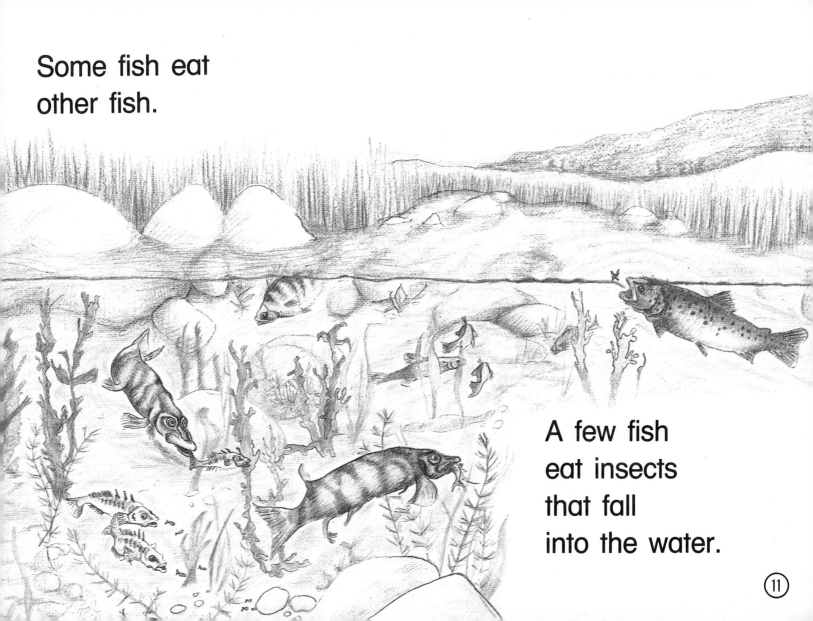

A few fish
eat insects
that fall
into the water.

Different fish
have different ways
of protecting themselves
from enemies.

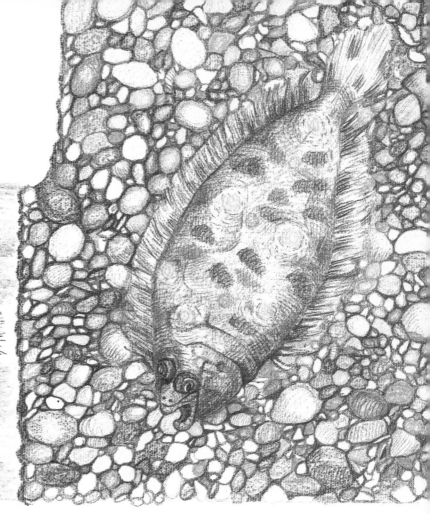

Some have sharp spines.

Some change
color.

One carries
a sword!

The electric eel
can give
its enemy
a shock.

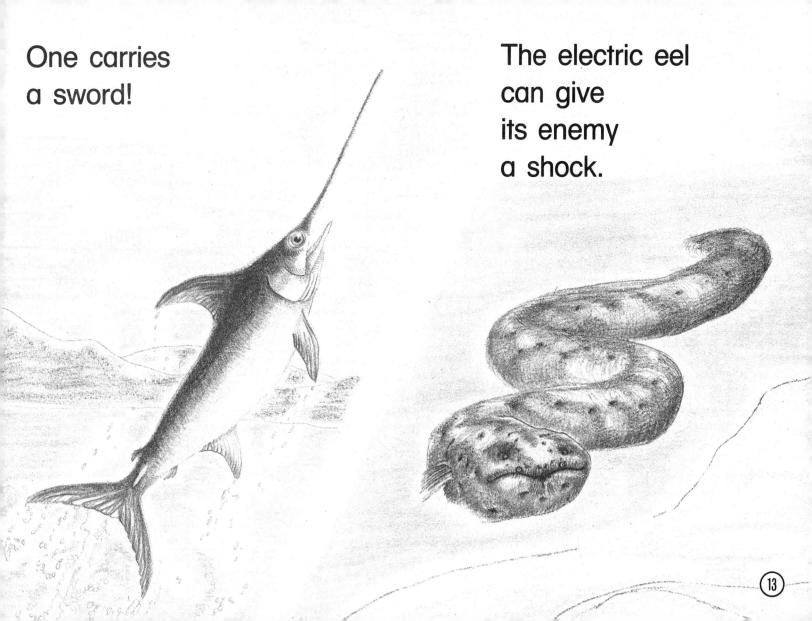

QUIZ

Ask your friend these questions. . .

Does a fish have a  ?

Is a  cold-blooded?

What are the fish's fins for?

Do fish have lungs?

How do fish get oxygen?

Where does plankton grow?

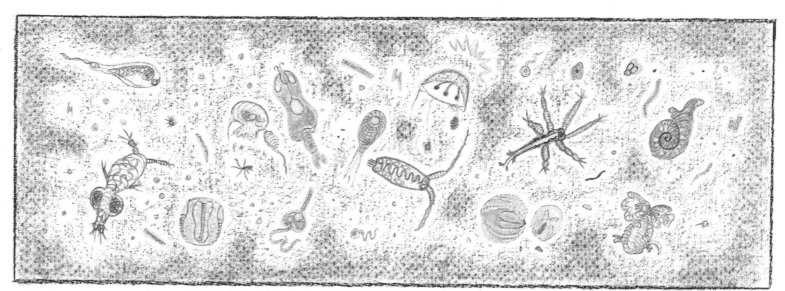

Plankton is made up of tiny plants and animals.

Some things to do by yourself or as a group

1. Paint a large picture of an underwater scene. It could be sea water or fresh water.

Draw and color in as many different types of fish as you can find in a reference book.

Then cut them out and paste them onto your painting. Write in their names.

(Be careful not to have fresh water fish swimming in salty sea water, or the other way around!)

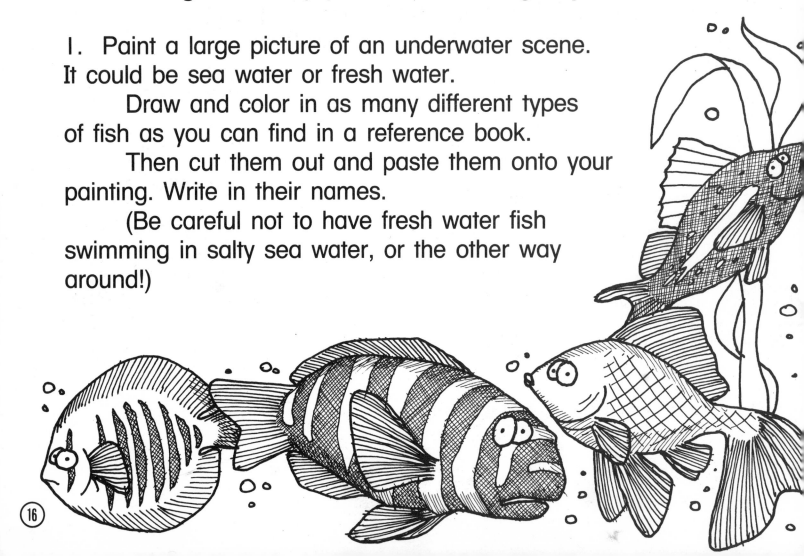